Kaleed-e-Dil

Key to Heart - Different Shades of Life & Love

Anooj Gupta

BookLeaf Publishing
India | USA | UK

Made with ❤ on the BookLeaf Publishing Platform
www.bookleafpub.in
www.bookleafpub.com

Dedication

I dedicate this book to all the souls who have ever felt my words, who understood my pain, love, and struggles. These poems are the result of experiences that have deeply resided in my heart and mind. The complexities of life, the simplicity of love, the pain of betrayal, and the depth of philosophy – all have guided my pen in this journey. I am forever grateful to my family, friends, and everyone who stood by me, encouraging me to move forward.

I hope that these poems find a place in your hearts and offer a new perspective to your thoughts.

इस पुस्तक को मैं उन सभी आत्माओं को समर्पित करता हूँ जिन्होंने कभी मेरे शब्दों को महसूस किया, जिन्होंने मेरे दर्द, प्रेम, और संघर्ष को समझा। यह रचनाएँ उन्हीं अनुभवों का परिणाम हैं जो मेरे दिल और दिमाग में गहरे बसे हैं। जीवन की जटिलताओं, प्रेम की सरलता, विश्वासघात की पीड़ा और दर्शन की गहराई – सभी ने मेरी कलम को मार्गदर्शन दिया है। इस यात्रा में साथ देने के लिए मैं अपने परिवार, मित्रों और उन सभी लोगों का आभारी हूँ जिन्होंने मेरे साथ खड़े होकर मुझे आगे बढ़ने की प्रेरणा दी।

आशा है कि ये कविताएँ आपके दिल में भी गहरे स्थान बनाएं और आपकी सोच को कुछ नया दृष्टिकोण प्रदान करें।

Thank you || धन्यवाद

Preface

Poetry is a form of expression where unsaid emotions and thoughts find their voice. This book is a collection of those emotions and experiences within me, which I have tried to shape into words. The diversity of life, love, betrayal, struggle, and philosophy—these have been the core themes of my writing.

The poems compiled in this book are not just a part of my personal journey but are also for those who have ever felt these emotions. Each poem is a story, an experience, a thought that, in some form, may resonate with everyone's life.
In the 35 years of my life, I have tried to convey through these poems everything that I have experienced. Here, there is the tenderness of love, the intensity of betrayal, and the depth of philosophy.

I hope these poems reach your heart and leave a special imprint in your life. The inspiration behind writing this book came from a deep place in my soul, and I sincerely hope that it reaches you as well.

Thank you.

कविता, शब्दों का ऐसा रूप है जिसमें अनकहे भावनाओं और विचारों को व्यक्त किया जा सकता है। यह पुस्तक मेरे भीतर के उन भावनाओं और अनुभवों का संग्रह है, जिन्हें शब्दों में ढालने का प्रयास किया है। जीवन की विविधता, प्रेम, विश्वासघात, संघर्ष, और दर्शन, ये सभी विषय मेरे लेखन के केंद्र में रहे हैं।

इस पुस्तक में संकलित कविताएँ न केवल मेरी व्यक्तिगत यात्रा का हिस्सा हैं, बल्कि यह उन सबके लिए हैं जिन्होंने कभी इन भावनाओं को महसूस किया है। हर कविता एक कहानी है, एक अनुभव है, एक विचार है, जो किसी न किसी रूप में हर इंसान के जीवन का हिस्सा हो सकता है।

मेरे जीवन के 35 वर्षों के इस सफर में जो कुछ भी मैंने अनुभव किया, उसे मैंने इन कविताओं के माध्यम से आप तक पहुँचाने की कोशिश की है। यहाँ प्रेम की कोमलता है, विश्वासघात की तीव्रता है, और दर्शन की गहराई भी है।

मुझे उम्मीद है कि ये कविताएँ आपके दिल तक पहुँचेंगी, और आपके जीवन में कुछ नया, कुछ विशेष छाप छोड़ेंगी। इस पुस्तक को लिखते समय मुझे जो प्रेरणा मिली, वह मेरी आत्मा से गहरी थी, और मैं आशा करता हूँ कि यह प्रेरणा आप तक भी पहुंचे।

धन्यवाद।

Acknowledgements

Kaleed-e-Dil is more than a collection of words—it is a soul poured onto paper, a journey through the countless shades of life and love, inked with both trembling and triumph.

I owe this journey, first and foremost, to **my wife, Arti**—the quiet anchor to my chaos, the calm in every storm, and the heartbeat behind many unspoken verses. Your unwavering support and belief in my words have been the light guiding me through the darkest edits and the longest nights.

To **my family—Maa (Veena Ji) and Papa (Naresh Ji)**, whose blessings carry the fragrance of every poem; **my elder brother (Ankit)**, who taught me to stand tall; and **my sister-in-law (Ritika)**, whose warmth feels like poetry in itself—thank you for being my constants. Your love is the rhythm beneath every rhyme.

A very special shoutout to the tiniest co-authors of my joy—**my daughter Advika** and **my nephew Rian**. Your giggles, questions, and pure eyes have reminded me to always write with wonder and live with softness.

To the readers holding this book now—thank you. You've just turned the key. The door to the heart is open.

With love,
Anooj Gupta
IG- ChildhoodOfPoet
Writting Name - Saheb

1. Khaamoshiyaan, Kaghaz, Kaleed

Kabhi kabhi mohabbat ka kaghaz jal jaata hai,
Kaleed mil jaati hai, par dil tala ban jaata hai...
Aur khaamoshiyaan... wo toh sirf likhne ke kaam aati hain...!!

----XX-----

Teri muskurahat ki khaamoshiyaan thi kuch khaas,
Jo dil ke kaghaz pe likh gayi ek udaas pyaas,
Main khud se juda hokar bhi tujh mein tha bas gaya,
Teri aankhon mein likha tha koi raaz..!!

Har din ek nayi dastaan, har raat ek nayi misaal,
Tere saath waqt ka har lamha lagta tha kamaal,
Kaleed thi tu us duniya ki jahan sirf main tha,
Aur mohabbat thi meri be-misaal..!!

Chaand raaton mein, dil-e-kalam se likhe the humne vaade,

Teri saanson ki khaamoshiyaan bhi keh jaati thi iraade,
Ek pal mein tu gale lagti, doosre mein door ho jaati,
Phir bhi har baat mein pyaar ke the saaz-o-naade..!!

Kaleed thi tu, mere dil ki, par kisi aur ke dil ka tala khola,
Emaan-e-wafa thi tujh per, Ziyadah sab se jahan mein,
Per tere zazbaton mein ab vo mehak na thi,
Teri ankhon mein ab voh chehak na thi
Khaamoshiyaan bol uthi thi, tere jhooth ki zubaan mein,
Musukuarhat thi chehre per beshakmere , per andar se
tha toota aur khokla

Us gali se tha guzrta jahan teri yaadon ka tha aangan,
Kaghaz ke tukdon pe likhe the. jahan ab sirf bewafaai ke
geet har kadam,
Kaleed dhoondta hoon ab bhi tere dil ke kone mein,
Par milti sirf khaamoshiyaan, chubhne wali, khati jaise
narangam..!!

Aaj bhi tere liye likhta hoon, khaamoshiyon se baat karta
hoon,
Kaghaz ki jholi mein dard bhar ke raat tey karta hoon,
Mujhe chhod gayi tu us mod par jahan khud se mulaqat
hoti hai,
Kaleed ab bhi paas hai, par tera dil ab har pal khojta
hoon..!!

2. एक ही अनंत

जटाओं से बहता गंगाजल, हर सूरत में धार है,
चुप बैठा जो शमशानों में, वही जीवन का सार है,
तांडव भी है, शांति भी है, वही राग-रूद्र का तार है,
जो हर रूप में समाया है, वो शिव ही तो सरकार है।

वो भस्म रचाए भाल पे, न कोई मुकुट, न श्रृंगार है,
कंठ में विष को थामे जो, वही सृष्टि का आधार है,
कभी अघोरी, कभी भोला, कभी त्रिपुरारी अवतार है,
कभी निराकार की परिभाषा, कभी साकार उपकार है।

अर्धनारीश्वर जो बना, प्रेम का वो विस्तार है,
शक्ति-संग से जीवन का, हर तत्व समाहित यार है,
ना नर, ना नारी, ना देह की सीमा, बस इक पारावार है,
जिसमें लय भी है, विलय भी है, और सृजन भी बारम्बार है।

नटराज की पायल बोले जब, समय खुद भी लाचार है,
हर क़दम पे जो नाचे वो, रचता ब्रह्मांड अपार है,
तांडव जब करता है शिव, थरथरता संसार है,
उसकी आंखों में जलता है, काल से भी बड़ा विचार है।

कभी भैरव बनके आया, तो भय भी चरणों में हार है,
कभी आशुतोष बन जाए, तो हर वरदान तैयार है,
ना मांगता कुछ अपने लिए, वो सबसे बड़ा उदार है,
मन की थकान मिटाए जो, वो अंतर्मन का प्यार है।

--XX--

"Sahab" भी लिखे जो शब्द सजे, हर हर के उस पार है,
शब्दों से क्या बाँधूँ उसको, जो मौन का भी आकार है।

3. Kabhi Yoon Bhi To ho - Part 1

Kabhi yoon bhi to ho,
Darya ka sahil ho,
Mera dil ghayal ho,
Pooray chand ki raat ho,
Tanhayi aur mera sath ho,
Sagar ki lehre mujhse door jaye,
Aur tum aao!!

Kabhi yoon bhi to ho,
PariyoN ki koi mehfil ho.
Hum usme shamil ho,
Koi tumhari baat ho,
Jab meri muskurahat mere sath ho,
Main unhe tumahara naam batau,
Aur tum aao..!!

Kabhi yoon bhi to ho,
Yeh narm mulayem thandi hawayen,
Ye pyar jaisi gheri fizayein,

Jab ghar say tumharay guzrain,
Tumhare badan ko chumein,
Tumhari khusbu churayen,
Meri rooh , mere zehen tak ley aayen,
Aur tum yun aao..!!

Kabhi yoon bhi to ho,
Sooni har manzil ho,
Jiska na ho koi rasta,
Koi na mere sath ho,
Na kisi ko ho mujhse vasta,
Mere aansuon mein tumhara naam aye,
Aur tum aao!!

Kabhi yoon bhi to ho,
Yeh badal aisa toot kay barsay,
Jaise samundar ki lehrein sahil se milne ko tarsay,
Mere dil ki tarah milnay ko,
Tumhara dil bhi tarsay,
Tum ghar say niklo, Tumhein meri sanson mein apna
naam mile,
Aur tum aao!!

Kabhi yoon bhi to ho,
Tanhai ho, Ruswayi nahi,
Dil ho,Dhadkanein nahi,
Zindagi ho, Per sansein nahi,

Tum ho, Sirf tumhari yaadien nahi,
Boondain hoon, Barsaatein nahi,
Apne man mein tum mujhe pukaro,
Aur main aao!!

4. Bechain Hai Jo, Woh Azaadi Se Hai

You may leave, but my strength remains untamed,
I rise from the silence, with every question unchained.
Even in my quiet, there's a fire that won't fall,
For every step, every struggle, is my own call.

--XX--

Tum jaa chuke ho to kya, yeh koi bawaal thodī hai,
Main toot ke bhi muskurā duñ, yeh kamaal thodī hai.

Jo aaj chup hoon to ye samjho mat ke haar gaya,
Ye khamoshi to hai, magar behaal thodī hai.

Wo paas rahe ya door, mujhe farq kya padta hai,
Tamannaon ke sheher mein ab bhi ujāl thodī hai.

Savaalon ka silsila to rahega zindagi bhar,
Magar mujhse na poochho ke har sawaal, sawaal thodī hai.

Khudā ki rehmat mein agar kuchh saath mil bhi jaaye,
Toh samjho, mere sajde ka hi kamaal thodī hai.

Us ne jo aankhon se baat ki, wo bhi ik dastaan thi,
Lafz toh zaroori hain, har baar misaal thodī hai.

"Sahab" aaj us mod par hai jahan sab kuch keh bhi sakte hai,
Par har jazbaat ko bolna behaal thodī hai.

5. Musalsal Safar

Bachpan ka har khwab tha ek adhoora safar, chhoti
chhoti khwahishon ka asar chala gaya
Pandra saal ki umr mein thaak ke, maa ka anchal chhod
kar shehar chala gaya

Gudiyon ke khel, school ki ghanti, sab kuchh tha ek
sapna bas nazar chala gaya
Jismein tha rangon ka jahan, wo to waqt ke saath hi
bikhhar chala gaya

Har Eid purani qameez mein guzri, naye jooton ka toh
na kabhi khabar chala gaya
Logo ne kaha chhota hai, lekin zindagi ka bojh toh bada
hunar chala gaya

Pehli mohabbat thi, magar jaat-paat, paison ne sab kuch
udar chala gaya
Main aankhon mein sapna leke tha, woh bas mere halaat
dekh kar utar chala gaya

Shehar mein tha bheed ka raag, aur main tanha ek dagar chala gaya
Lekin har thokar se seekh kar, main apne hone ka safar chala gaya

Roti mili, neend chhin gayi, armaan har din kamar chala gaya
Phate kapdon mein bhi maangta raha izzat, aur aakhir main samar chala gaya

Aaj maa ke pairon ke neeche hai jannat, aur baap ki aankhon mein guroor chala gaya
Bhai behno ke chehre pe muskan hai, har kami ka shukr chala gaya

"Sahab" ke alfaaz the kabhi bheegte kaghazon mein, aaj kitaabon mein sitar chala gaya
Dil to wohi hai lekin ab har dard ka rang, ek shayar chala gaya

6. Kabhi Yoon Bhi To Ho - Part 2

Kabhi yoon bhi to ho,
Teen pyaalein, aur khumaar ho,
Taron se bhara aasmaan ho,
Aur chaand meri aankhon mein basay,
Tumhari hasi se rangon ka jahan ho,
Phir se ek baar, yun dua ho,
Aur tum aao!!

Kabhi yoon bhi to ho,
Ghazlon ki raat ho,
Kahin kisi khwab ki baat ho,
Hum saath me yun sath ho,
Tumhare bina yeh duniya sunson ho,
Phir bhi teri khushboo mein mera aasra ho,
Aur tum aao!!

Kabhi yoon bhi to ho,
Koi rangin mehfil ho,
Jahan dhadkanon ki gawaiyon ka chaaron or silsila ho,

Jahaan sirf tumhara saath ho,
Aur meri gulab jaisi baatein hon,
Aur tum aao!!

Kabhi yoon bhi to ho,
Jab khushbuon mein tumhara saath ho,
Waqt ki rahon mein tum meri aawaaz ho,
Tumhari khushiyo ka jahan ho,
Aur mere khwab mein tumhara aangan ho,
Har mousam mein milein yun sanam, ho,
Aur tum aao!!

Har raat zara marta raha main

Yun ankhon se dil-e-gam bayan karta raha main,
Har roz zara se jyada marta raha main,
Khush-numa hokar dekhliya maine bhi,
Teri hi khushali ke liye darta raha main,
Tune chor jana munasib samjha,
Toot kar bhi khwab mein jeeta raha main,
Mujhe lafzon ke fasane ,shabdon ke tarane nahi ate,
Tujhe yun nazmon mein likh, bikharta raha main,
Ki maine chipa rakhe the kitne ashq in ankhon mein,
Teri didon mein panah le, bas sanvarta raha main,
Na ho chahe tu ruu-ba-ruu ab mujhse,
Per teri mohabbat ki mehak mein sajta raha main,
Har raat zara se jyada marta raha main,
Har raat zara se jyada marta raha main..!!

8. Aurat: IkhtiyaaR Ka Naam

"'Raqeeb' sun lo, ab silsilay badalne wale hain,"
Aurat apne hone ka matlab samajhne lagi hai, aur kehti hai

"She walks on fire and still smiles.
Turns her tears into strength.
She bends history, shatters silence, and dares patriarchy —
And then... she simply says:
I am not less than anyone."

--XX--

Naam mera aurat hai, zakhm bhi seh jaati hoon,
Chhup - chhup ke roti hoon, par na kabhi ghabraati hoon,
Tooti hoon kai baar, magar har baar nayi banti hoon,
Main mitti hoon, har baar phir se saj jaati hoon..!!

Raatein bhi meri, chaand bhi mera, sab kuch roshan kar doon,
Jis din main bolti hoon, andheron mein bijli bhar doon,
Jhuki thi pehle dua mein, ab uthi hoon savaal ban ke.
Umadta Toofan hoon, hawaon ka rukh bhi palat kar doon..!!

Mere aansuon ko kamzori ka naam mat dena,
Yeh toh taqat hain, inka hisaab mat lena.
Main bhanwar mein thi tab bhi, kinare tak le aayi khud ko,
Tufanon mein bhi chali hoon, mujhko fir dubane ki chahh mat lena..!!

Main sirf ek rishta nahi, main soch hoon, ujala hoon,
Zamaane ke liye khud ek naya sawala hoon,
Main woh hoon jo chhupkar bhi jagti rehti hai raaton mein,
Tareekh ki kitaabon mein likha ek faisala hoon..!!

Main aaj ke zamane ki tasveer hoon, misaal hoon,
Jab bolti hoon, har lafz mein inquilab ka haal hoon,
Main wo aawaaz hoon jo ab sirf naghme nahi likhti,
Main jazbaat nahi, ab poora ka poora ek sawal hoon..!!

9. Zikr-e-Khamoshi

Ik khud se mulaqat ka hi toh raaz milta hai,
Sannaton mein jo gum ho jaaye, wo saaz milta hai.

"It's in the silence where the soul begins to hum,
Not in scriptures, nor in voices,
but in the echo of your own breath,
you find the God that lives within you..!!

--XX--

Jab chehra dhundhla ho jaye, aur soch bhi ho dhundli-dhundli,
Tabhi dil ke aangan mein ek naya aaina saaz milta hai.

Shorr ke sheher se nikal kar, jab tu khamoshi chhoota hai,
Ek aawaaz andar se, bin kahe, har baat milta hai.

Na mandir, na masjid, na kathaa, na koi kitaab,
Jab aankhon ko band karein, tab khuda paas milta hai.

Saans lene ka fan bhi seekhna padta hai dosto,
Jab har saans mein ek naya jazbaat milta hai.

Bichhad ke har ek shikayat se, chhod ke har ek nafrat ko,
Aakhir mein sirf khud se ek behtareen andaaz milta hai.

Safar koi door ka toh hai hi nahi yeh raaz-e-hayat,
Jo khud mein kho jaaye, use har manzil khaas milta hai.

Sahab, har khwaab mein mat dhoondo khushi ka raasta,
Kabhi ashq bhi ankhon ko ek noor sa milta hai..!!

10. वो जो समय की ज़रूरत हुआ

वो जब आया,
तो मत्स्य बनकर समंदर की गहराइयों से
एक नाव लेकर निकला,
जिसमें दुनिया की आख़िरी उम्मीद बैठी थी–
बीज, जानवर, ऋषि, और डर।
वो सिर्फ़ बचाने नहीं आया था,
वो शुरुआत था।

जब धरती कांपी,
पर्वत डगमगाए,
तो वो कूर्म बनकर
पेट पे पहाड़ उठाए खड़ा रहा–
एक पीठ थी,
जिस पर देव भी टिका करते थे।

वो कीचड़ में उतरा,
वराह बनकर,
ना सजी-धजी मूर्ति था,
ना मंदिर का दीप।
वो था जो गंदगी में भी

धरती को गोद में लेकर बाहर लाया।

स्तंभ फटा,
और उसमें से निकला एक क्रोध–
ना मनुष्य था, ना शेर।
नरसिंह था–
वो आकार जो न्याय के लिए
रूपों से आज़ाद था।

कभी आया,
तो वामन बनकर,
छोटे क़दमों में आकाश नाप लिया।
भिक्षा में ब्रह्मांड माँग लिया,
और फिर भी मुस्कुराया–
जैसे विनम्रता ही असली विजय हो।

राम था–
जो राजकुमार होकर भी जंगल चला गया।
जिसने प्रेम त्यागा,
पर धर्म नहीं।
जो हर बार
धनुष उठाने से पहले
मन की गांठें खोलता था।

फिर आया कृष्ण–
हँसता हुआ, बांसुरी में छिपी रणभूमि।
वो जो रास में भी रणनीति जानता था,

जो मां के हाथों माखन खाता था,
और अर्जुन को गीता सुनाता था।
वो खेलता भी था,
और युद्ध में मार्ग भी दिखाता था।

अभी एक बाक़ी है–
कल्कि।
जो आएगा–
जब शब्द थक जाएँगे,
जब न्याय सिर्फ़ किताबों में मिलेगा,
जब तलवार की ज़रूरत फिर होगी
सच्चाई के लिए।
तब वो सफ़ेद घोड़े पर आएगा,
और सृष्टि की साँस फिर से गहरी होगी।

11. Thak Gaya Hai Voh

Thak gaya h voh, per kahega nahi,
Kamzor jitna marzi hua ho, per dikhayega nahi,

Sabke Sapnon ko pura karna h use, daud raha hai,
Ruk kar ghav per mehrum lagayega nahi,
Kher waqt bhi kaha hai, pahle hi waqt se bahut peeche h voh,

Chahe shartir kitna ho voh,
Bigadte Halaton ke aage seedha h voh,

Duniya jitna marzi neecha dikhaye,
Kadwe waqt ke aage, meetha pal h voh,

Koshish kar sakta h, bas vohi kare ja raha h voh,
Sab badlega ek din uske liye, is umeed per
Bas badta ja raha h voh, badta ja raha h voh..!!

12. Apne Mayar Se Neeche

Apne mayar se neeche toh main aane se raha,
Pyasa rahu chahe per paimane se neeche toh main aane se raha,
Kaha jau main, faisla kar e-khuda,
Uski ibadat bhi nahi chhoott thi,
Aur sara jeevan, mera dil sirf maikhane mein raha..!!

Aaj sab ko chor ke apne pe bharosa karliya Maine,
Jo main marne Ko tha use zinda karliya Maine,
Tu aaj bharose layak na lagta mujhe,
Teri ibadat se palat dusri taraf man kar liya maine,
Zinda h mohabbat aaj bhi teri,
Dil ka sare-e-kam katal karliya maine ..!!

Mar gaya voh jo tujh per marta tha,
Dard tujhe hota, ankhon mein aansu bharta tha,
Tere shami sawalon ne ishq khokhla kar diya uska,
Varna har pal vo apni jaan tujh per chidakta tha
Aaj duniya mein dhoke bazi ke mele hai,
Aisa Bepanah pyar to bhala pehle bhi kaun karta tha,

Tune rulaya use har pal apni tadap mein,
Varna khushiyon ka mehakma uska kabhi kam na padta tha,
Aaj tere intezar ka diya bhuja diya usne apne akhri saas se,
Mar gaya aaj voh, jo humesha tujh per marta tha..!!

13. न जवाब, न गिला

ख़ामोशियाँ भी बोलती हैं अब, जब आवाज़ नहीं होती,
कभी कभी सबसे साफ़ जवाब वही होता है – जो कहा ही नहीं जाता।,

--XX--

हाल कुछ ऐसा है इन दिनों, कि ख़ुशी की भी चुप कहानी है,
हँसी तो है होठों पे, पर आँखों में धूप पुरानी है,
रूठा-सा साज़ है दिल का, पर बजती वही रवानी है,
हर लम्हे में उजाला है, पर फिर भी थोड़ी वीरानी है।

रूह में कोई शोर मचा है, पर लफ़्ज़ों में थकान सी है,
हर बात अधूरी लगती है, जैसे रातें बे-ज़ुबानी हैं,
कहना तो बहुत कुछ है अब भी, पर खामोश निगाहें बानी हैं,
हर जुमला किसी इंतज़ार में है, हर सांस में कहानी है।

यादें हैं जैसे धूप छाँव में चलती शाम सुहानी है,
पर उन रातों में अब चाँदनी नहीं, बस कुछ पुरानी निशानी है,
तूने जो आँखों से पढ़ लिया, वो मेरी सबसे बड़ी रवानी है,
तू समझा भी सब कुछ ख़ामोशी से, ये इश्क़ की मेहरबानी है।

ज़िंदगी आज भी सवाल सी है, ना कोई हल, ना कहानी है,
दिल की दराज़ों में रखे हैं ख़त, पर मुहर अब भी पुरानी है,
इश्क़ का कोई हिसाब नहीं, ना वज़न, ना कोई रवानी है,
बस महसूस होता है हर कोने में, जैसे तृप्यास नहीं पानी है।

14. बात सिर्फ़ इश्क़ की नहीं है

"साहब" ये जो शेर कहता है, आग से भी भारी है,
ये बग़ावत है उस रूह की, जो साज़िश में ख़ामोश नहीं रही है।

--XX--

हर बार महफ़िल नहीं बस एकतरफ़ा प्यार की है,
ये चीख़ है उस दिल की,जिसकी तन्हाई हद से पार की है,
टूटी है चुप्पी भी कई बार उसके अभिमान की है,
ये दास्तान किसी रोज़ रोज़ मरती जान की है।

हर बार ग़लती इबादत या भगवान की नहीं,
कभी बात उस इंसान की है जो हर बार हारा है,
जिसके सपनों की चिता जली है आँखों में,
और जुबां पर खामोशी सजा इनाम की है।

कभी तो सोचो वो स्वाभिमान कितना टूटा होगा,
जो झुक गया चौराहे पर भीड़ के बीच में,
और जिसको तमाशा बना दिया गया इश्क़ के नाम पर,
वो मोहब्बत नहीं, सज़ा किसी बयान की है।

कभी तो बात बढ़ते हुए घमंड की भी होती है,

जहाँ खुदा बनने लगे कोई, और खुदाई बाँटे,
पर उसको क्या पता कि आग हर बार परछाईं नहीं देखती,
जलती बस्ती उसी की है, जिसकी फ़ितरत शमशान की है।

अब ये मत कहना फिर कि वक़्त ही ख़राब था,
कभी तो आईना देखो, शक्ल भी जवाब की है,
हर ज़ुल्म पे तालियाँ क्यों बजीं हैं महफ़िल में,
कभी सोचना, ये साज़िश भी इंसान की है।

15. तू मेरी कच्ची उम्र का ख्वाब

"साहब" तुझे लिखते हुए भी कांप जाती है क़लम,
तू सिर्फ़ ख़्वाब नहीं, मेरी दुआओं का जवाब सा है।

--XX--

तू मेरी कच्ची उम्र का ख्वाब सा है,
मेरे हर अनसुलझे सवाल का जवाब सा है,
ज़िंदगी के बिखरे अंधेरों में आफ़ताब सा है,
तू मेरी कच्ची उम्र का ख्वाब सा है..!!

तू मेरी हर नाकाम कोशिश की जीत सा है,
मेरे आँखों के आँसुओं को हँसी में बदलने वाली रीत सा है,
तू जलते अंगारों में पानी का तालाब सा है,
तू मेरी कच्ची उम्र का ख्वाब सा है..!!

तू मेरे अनकहे शब्दों की शब्दमाला सा है,
तू हर समय जलने वाली प्यार का ज्वाला सा है,
तू काँटों से भरी दुनिया में गुलाब सा है,
तू मेरी कच्ची उम्र का ख्वाब सा है..!!

तू मेरी जिंदगी की चलती साँसों सा है,
धड़कन में छुपी बातों सा है,
तू हर अमावस्या की रात का महताब सा है,
तू मेरी कच्ची उम्र का ख्वाब सा है..!!

16. Chuppi bhari Cheekh

तुम बिन जो हालत है, वो शेरों में बयाँ नहीं होती,
घर की दीवारें पूछती हैं – ये तन्हा सिसकन कहाँ नहीं होती,
तेरी यादें अब भी चाय की तरह हर शाम में घुलती हैं,
पर बेचैनियों की शक्ल किसी दवाख़ाने में दवा नहीं होती।

कहने को तो सब ठीक है, पर नींदें नीलाम हो चुकी हैं,
तेरे बग़ैर हर साँस उधारी पे चल रही, सुकून ख़ामोश हो चुकी है,
कब्र सा सन्नाटा है इस दिल में, पर लोग पूछते हैं – कैसी तबीयत है?
क्या बताएँ, तेरे बिना अब ज़िन्दगी भी इत्तिफ़ाक़ नहीं होती।

उसने मोहब्बत को मोल लिया, अहसास को सौदा समझ लिया,
हमने जो परवाह की, उसे रोक-टोक का झगड़ा समझ लिया,
हमने चुप रह के इश्क़ निभाया, उसने चिल्ला के 'ज़िद' कह दिया,
और फिर अपनी नई मोहब्बत को ही, बेदाग़ वफ़ा समझ लिया।

आज भी उसे गुरूर है अपने अफ़साने की शोहरत पर,
हमने तो नाम तक मिटा दिया – उसकी राहत पर, उसकी ज़हमत पर,
वो जिसे परी समझ बैठे हैं, उसे हमने आइना दिखा दिया,
जिसे उसने इश्क़ कहा, उसे हमने बग़ावत का नाम दे दिया।

17. माँ, तेरी गोद से दूर हूँ मैं

" अंश" हूँ तेरा, और तुझमें ही पूरा होता हूँ मैं,
दुनिया चाहे जो भी कहे, बस तुझमें ही सच्चा होता हूँ मैं

--XX--

यहाँ मांगती है, छाया, भारी धूप,
दिखता है मौसम का हर सुहाना रूप,
है सब खाने को यहाँ, और पीने को भी,
है सब रहने को यहाँ, और जीने को भी,
पर तभी माँ तेरे बिन अधूरा हूँ मैं,
सब होकर भी मेरे पास, न कभी पूरा हूँ मैं,
तेरे बिन मेरी माँ अधूरा हूँ मैं...!!

तू ही बता कैसे, तेरे बिन रहूँ,
लगता है सब खाली, जैसे शरीर बिन लहू,
ऐ माँ, यहाँ कोई भी नहीं है अपना,
कोई थामेगा मेरा हाथ दुख के समय, ये तो लगता है अब एक सपना,
बस एक तू ही तो है माँ, जिसने, मुझे रोता देख, हमेशा चुप कराया,
मेरे दुखों को खुशी में बदल, हमेशा पूरे दिल से हंसाया,
पर यहाँ तो मुझे लोग हंसता देख, पागल कहते हैं,
मुझे रोता हुआ देख ही, खुश रहते हैं..!!

पर न करना, ऐ माँ, तू मेरी फिक्र,
काटेगा आपका बच्चा, खुश रहकर, ये सफर,
आपकी डांट, आपके प्यार ने, जिंदगी का बहुत ज्ञान सिखाया है,
मुसीबतों से लड़कर, जीत सकू, इँतना काबिल बनाया है,
इसलिए न करना परवाह, मैं सब खेल जाऊंगा, जितनी बड़ी. चाहे हो मुश्किल, मैं सब झेल जाऊंगा!!

ऐ माँ, करता हूँ तुझसे प्यार बेतिहाश,
तेरे बिन ज़िंदगी है खाली, अधूरी है हर जगह,
जैसे, समुद्र बिन रेत, किसान बिन खेत,
बिन शाही-ए खत, बिन शरीरे-रक़्त,
तेरे बिन बहुत मुश्किल से गुजरता है ये वक्त,
कब खत्म होगा ये इंतज़ार का समय,
कब आपके गले लगकर हंसूंगा मैं,
बस अब और नहीं सहा जाता, आपके बिन,
अब और नहीं रहा जाता, आपके बिन,
जल्द आपका सपना पूरा कर आ रहा हूँ मैं,
ना करना चिंता, बस पढ़ाई का ही ज्ञान पा रहा हूँ मैं,
सब पकड़कर जल्द आपकी शरण आऊंगा,
बस फिर अपना घर, आपके चरणों में ही बसाऊंगा..!!

18. Aakhri Koshish

'साहब' अब भी रखता है दिल में एक उम्मीद,
शायद लौट आए वो, बस इक बार कह दे "दोस्ती अभी ज़िंदा है"।

--XX--

Jaan kar , bhi najanae kyu hai ye anjaan, seher ,
Bahut mushkil se kat te hai din ke aath peher ,
Itne dost hokar bhi , nahi kat ta samay ,
Pata ni kis alag duniya mein , kho gaya hu main ,
Sab hokar bhi , sab lagta hai adhoora ,
Jaise bane ho mithe chawal , bin bhoora ,
Jaise bin raqt , sharir na hota poora ,
Vaise hi bin tum , hu main adhoora..!!

Najane kyu chup hai mera dimag , mera dil ,
Chahkar bhi , nahi pa raha hu sabse ghul-mil ,
Rehta hu sabke sath , karta hu sabse baat ,
Per najanae kyu tabhi lagta hai ,
jaise hu main akela har din , har raat ,
Najane kab dhund paunga in sawalon ka jawab ,

Najane kab milega , in halaton ka illaz..!!

Yu tu chand bhi bhatakta hai raat bhar ,
Main jo bhatak gaya to baat kya ,
Royi na aankhein jo takiye se lipatkar ,
Vo hoga kala din , vo mere liye raat kaha ,
Rahegi tanahai tab tak , mera akelapan ,
Jab tak nah ho tumhari yaad vaha ,
Yu to chand bhi bhatakta hai raat bhar ,
Main jo bhatak gaya to baat kya..!!

Tumhare bin jeena lagta hai adhoora ,
Jaise khatam hogaya ho khoon , sharir se poora ,
Tum bin, har samay lagte hai dil per zakham ,
Jinke upar ni karta asar koi bhi mahram ,
Man karta hai roklu , kardun in sansoon ko khatam ,
Karlu apne sharir ko is judai ki aag mein bhasam ,
Per najane rok leti hai mujhe , kaunsi Shakti ,
Kehti hai , ji zindagi , aur nibha apne farzon ki bhakti..!!

Yu tu patte bhi girte hai ped se patjhar mein,
Per unke jeene ka maksad nahi toot ta ,
Pani ki boodein bhi girti hai aasman se ,
Per unka sparsh nahi choot ta ,
Subah ka bhoola ghar laut aye ,
To vo bhi nahi kehlaya jata bhoola ,
Har jeev musibaton ke baad , fir karta hai shuruvaat ,

Kyunki unke jeen ka irada nahi toot ta ,
To kya unhe dekh hum bhi kar sakte hai ek aur koshish ,
Kyunki maine to suna tha , dosti ka rishta tode nahi toot ta..!!

De do mujhe ek mauka , dost ban ne ka ,
Ek mauka , apni galtiyon se bhar nikalne ka ,
Dosti hogi pavitre jaise ki ganga jal ,
Launga tumhare liye sari khushiyan ,
Na hoga dukho ka ek bhi pal ,
Na hoga dukho ka ek bhi pal..!!

19. Echoes of the Old Me

It's been a month since silence grew,
Where once your laughter softly blew,
Now every breeze brings back a hue—
Of you... just you... only you.

I sit where shadows sip the day,
And still hear words you used to say,
They cling to time, they drift, they sway,
But never choose to fade away.

I've never loved this deep, this wide,
Even when pain chose to reside,
Though truth and hurt walked side by side,
My heart still held you, arms open wide.

So much I kept, unsaid, unheard,
Like poems locked without a word,
Why did you leave, without a third—
Page of us, unwritten, blurred?

I still recall your parting gaze,
That quiet burn, that misty haze,
I never knew those silent rays
Would turn to night and end our days.

If time could break and bend for me,
I'd steal back nights of misery,
Undo the faults that shouldn't be—
And hold you close, not memory.

The mirror shows what's left to see,
A stranger where I used to be,
You took more than just "you" from me...
I miss you most—
the old, whole Me.

20. Letters Never Sent

Don't twist my silence like a thread,
Your words still echo things unsaid,
Each smile you wore, now softly shed–
Like wilted petals turning red.

You come and go like shifting sand,
Yet leave your touch across my hand,
I built a world where we could stand–
But your love was always secondhand.

My heart's not meant for reckless play,
It's not a dice you throw away,
You leave, then write, then go astray–
And still expect me here to stay.

Don't bend my hopes to suit your art,
Don't tear these dreams and call it smart,
This isn't love when worlds fall apart–
You're playing games with someone's heart.

I bled my truth in every part,
And still you carved a moving chart,
This isn't fair, this isn't art—
So don't fold love like paper, heart.

21. The Journey of Solitude

What does it mean when silence speaks,
When the soul is bruised but never seeks,
A touch to heal, a voice to reach,
What does it mean when love feels weak?

When the moon's shine seems far away,
And the stars refuse to come and stay,
When words are lost, and hearts decay,
What does it mean when night holds sway?

When the echoes of your name are faint,
And the air feels colder, filled with restraint,
When hope becomes the smallest saint,
What does it mean when hearts can't paint?

In this emptiness, I stand alone,
Searching for a place I can call home,
A soul adrift in realms unknown,
What does it mean when love is thrown?

The days grow long, the nights unkind,
In the stillness, what do I find?
A hollow echo, a restless mind,
What does it mean to be left behind?

22. Couplets & Quatrain

Jo tu nahi toh yeh , Mukammal na ho sakegi,
Nashe ke bin , Sharab ki kya ehmiyat..!!

--XX--

Ek tu kya gaya ke poora qafila gaya
Zudai ki aag ne sukun ka ped jala diya
Jab riyasat se dil ki rani kuch pal ko fariq hui
Kya rona fir takht gaya ya qila giya

--XX--

Mohabbat mein mila kya,
Khoya bhi sab, ab bacha kya,
Dil bhi gaya, samay bhi, na bachi ab izzat,
Zamane ka sawal h ki luta kya hai,
Chahha use e'-jeevan toot kar maine,
Puchta h voh ki tune kiya kya hai...!!

--XX--

Karvatein badli raat bhar,
Har taraf bas tumhari Yaad ayi,
Din aya raat ayi, Na ayi jo,
Neend humein na ek raat ayi,
Dard aya, Aansu aye,
Na aya tu, na teri koi baat ayi,
Dil kehta raha teri hai voh,
Per humare hisse sirf teri yaad ayi.!!

--XX--

Khushiyon se bhara mauhal tha jeevan mein,
Farebi ishq ne jakad liya humein,
Vo khas h humare liye, ye jatate jatate,
Humne khud ko aam karliya..!!

--XX--

Dilli jaise sard sheher mein,
Bas teri garam bahinen apna aagaar hai,
Duniya jitni bewafa ho chahe,
Akhri saans tak humein sirf tera aitbaar hai..!!

--XX--

Haq sabne jamaya ,

Nibhaya rishta sirf chunindon ne,
Jeevan mein vo sab na paya,
Jo dikhaya khwabon ke parindon ne,
Tum, main aur hum sab chale jayenge ek din,
Jeelo har pal ko, khushiyon se,
Na maro har roz dukho k gintiyon mein..!!

--XX--

Ek samay per tumhe apna khas bhi chodna hoga
Khud Jeevan ka khud se jeene ki aas ko bhi chodna hoga
Kabhi sath, kabhi judai, Kabhi pyar , kabhi ladai
Duniya se ladte ladte tumhe apno ka hath bhi chodna hoga

--XX--

Kya beche jo fursat pa sake, ae zindagi
Sab kuch toh nilami mein hai,
Karne ko toh sab kiya, hui hasil per asafalta hi,
Shayad apni kismat bhi charan Seema ki nakami mein hai..!!

--XX--

Sari Umar karte rahe vo khidamat meri,
Jab main kabil hua , toh unki ichhayien mar gayi,

Jab tak samajh aya ki vastu nahi mera pyar hai unki icha

,

Tab tak mere sir per se chat hi gir gayi..!!

--XX--

Bin umeed na sahi, per nakam toh hai,
Tere bin gam-e-bhari ho chahe, per shaam toh hai..!!

--XX--

Meri har kahani , Teri kahani hai,
Per man na behla kisi kahani se,
Do pal ka sukoon milta h, Per,
Bhujti nahi pyas, tujhe jeetne ki rujhani se,
Jawani ki rawani ho ya rawani ki jawani,
Meri har kahani khatam hogi sirf
Tere sath beeti kahani se..!!

--XX--

Akelapan ko bhi tanhai mehsus hui ho jaise,
Intezar ko bhi muntazir rehna pada ho jaise,
Dil-e-dhadkan gaa rahi tera naam yu,
Har ek saans mein Teri yaad ayi ho jaise..!!

--XX--

Ya toh apne dil-e-ghar mein kaidi banade,
Ya apni bahon mein panah de..!!

--XX--

71% paani h dharti per, Fir bhi Dubaa har roz tere pyar mein,
Hasil beshak karli har school ko degree , Asli seekh DI sirf teri zudaai ki maar ne..!!

--XX--

Tum kamal karte ho,
Yun jo dhadkano ka
meri istemaal karte ho,
Gili zulfon ko jabhi
Patakteein ho hawa mein,
Maa kasam pure sheher ke
Dil mein bawaal karte ho..!!

--XX--

Parindo ki misaal de-dekar,
Apna shehar churdva diya,
Jitna bhi pyar tha dil mein,
Sab dhuein mein uda diya,

Beshak aaj rubaru hote h humse,
Teri jhukti aankhon ne sab kuch bata diya..!!

--XX--

Jaatein jaatein sari kamiyan ginvadi usne,
Najane kaunsi khoobi dekh kar fida the vo mujh per..!!

--XX--

Baap palta h bache ko nawab ki tarah,
Jo Kabhi khud bhi tha apni maa ka shehzada,
Ye shakhs apna lahu bech tumhari khwahishein khareed lata hai,
Na jaane kitne ehsaan bin kuch kahe asani se kar jata hai..!!